Suburbia

Suburbia

BY BILL OWENS

Straight Arrow Books

Library of Congress Catalog Card Number: 72-88835 √
ISBN: 0/87932/042/7 (paperbound)
0/87932/043/5 (clothbound)

First Printing

Stock Nos: 102042 (paper)
102043 (cloth)

Straight Arrow Books
625 Third Street
San Francisco, California 94107

Distributed by Quick Fox Inc.
33 West 60 Street
New York, New York 10023

Production: Planned Production

Printed in the United States of America by Rapport Printing Corp., New York

This book is about my friends and the world I live in.

In the fall of 1968 I began working as a photographer for the Livermore (California) <u>Independent</u>. My daily routine took me into the homes of hundreds of families and into contact with the social life of three suburban communities.

The people I met enjoy the life-style of the suburbs. They have realized the American Dream. They are proud to be home owners and to have achieved material success.

To me nothing seemed familiar, yet everything was very, very familiar. At first I suffered from culture shock. I wanted to photograph everything, thousands of photographs. Then slowly I began to put my thoughts and feelings together and to document Americans in Suburbia. It took two years.

The photos in this book express the lives of the people I know. The comments on each photograph are what the people feel about themselves.

Bill Owens

Summer 1972

To my wife Janet, because she sat home with Andrew and Eric; Alfred Heller for his understanding and support. And to the people of the Livermore Amador Valley. It's your book.

Suburbia

Sunday afternoon we get it
together. I cook the steaks and
my wife makes the salad.

I believe in women's liberation. I'm tired of the image of the woman who has the most sanitary toilet bowl, the cleanest floor and the brattiest kids as the supermother. I want to be able to change with my children and to change with my life as I grow older. Staying at home and taking care of the kids doesn't help.

Once you hit the Freeway you
can be in San Francisco in
forty minutes.

Every year I go to my mother-
in-law's for Thanksgiving and
every year I swear I'll never
do it again. But I always do,
do it again.

I bought the lawn in six-foot
rolls. It's easy to handle. I
prepared the ground and my
wife and son helped roll out
the grass. In one day you have
a front yard.

We moved up to a nicer house. We thought we'd do better, but the real estate man got us. Closing costs were supposed to be $295 but they turned out to be $750. They have you where they want you—you've already moved into the house.

People throw away a lot of good things: clothes, toys, broken toasters, record players and in the newer areas they throw out tables and chairs that don't fit in their new house. The ecology movement doesn't matter. I make over $250 in coke bottles. People here can't realize there are poor people in the world. They can't think about the needs of other people.

We lived in our house for a year without any living room furniture. We wanted to furnish the room with things we loved, not early attic or leftovers. Now we have everything but the pictures and the lamps.

Togetherness really exists in our family. My daughter and I operate the lunch room at the Valley Inn. My sons work part-time with their dad, hanging sheet-rock. And my eldest two sons work at the Gulf gas station on P St. We have 7 cars and 2 motorcycles in our family.

I find a sense of freedom in
the suburbs. . . . You assume
the mask of suburbia for out-
ward appearances and yet no
one knows what you really do.

My husband, Pat, has a
theory about watering our
newly seeded lawn. The water
has to trinkle from heaven and
fall like tender little rain drops
. . . otherwise the lawn won't
grow properly.

This isn't what we really want—the tract house, the super car, etc. . . . But as long as we are wound up in this high speed environment, we will probably never get out of it! We don't need the super car to be happy; we really want a small place in the country where you can breathe the air.

I get a lot of compliments on
the front room wall. I like Ital-
ian Syrocco floral designs over
the mantle. It goes well with
the Palos Verde rock fire-
place.

We've been married two
months and everything we
own is in this room.

We're home three weekends a year. Our camper is our real home. Being a member of the National Campers and Hikers Association gives our family the opportunity and the enjoyment of getting out of town every weekend . . . and to camp with other camper families.

The California garage today,
out of necessity, requires that
you move the cars out and the
tools in. To a point I enjoy
working in the garage, but I'd
rather be doing something
else.

We enjoy having these things.

Tuo-Tuo, our dog, is a very expensive household pet. It costs 30¢ a day to feed him—that's $109 a year—and $13 a month to have him groomed—that's $155 a year—not including the vet bill. We spend over $350 a year, but we don't care. We love him.

How can I worry about the
damned dishes when there are
children dying in Vietnam.

I enjoy giving a Tupperware
party in my home. It gives me
a chance to talk to my friends.
But really, Tupperware is a
homemaker's dream, you save
time and money because your
food keeps longer.

This is Valerie's world in miniature. She makes it what she wants it to be ... without war, racial hate or misunderstanding. Ken and Barbie (dolls) are man and woman rather than Mom and Dad. They enjoy living and having a camper truck is the good life. Today Valerie has the chicken pox and can't go out and play.

I was in the building and construction trade for 47 years before I retired. Since then I've taken up painting and have won many trophies. It gives me great satisfaction to know that some of my paintings are hanging in people's homes.

We have been married 35 years and for the last 5 years we have lived in the trailer park. We love it here because everything is convenient and the neighbors watch out for each other.

It's a great pleasure to watch yourself make love in the six dozen mirrors that line the ceilings and walls. I've spent a tremendous amount of thought and planning to get the total effect of the bedroom. It's fascinating to watch our friends' reactions to seeing the luxury and sensuousness of the room. Our bedroom is the most enjoyable room in the house.

We feel most people have the
wrong attitude towards sex,
that it's nasty and to be done
only in the dark. With us sex
takes care of itself.

I wanted Christina to learn
some responsibility for cleaning her room, but it didn't
work.

My baseball team is sponsor-
ed by Superior Tire of Hay-
ward—my dad owns Superior
Tire.

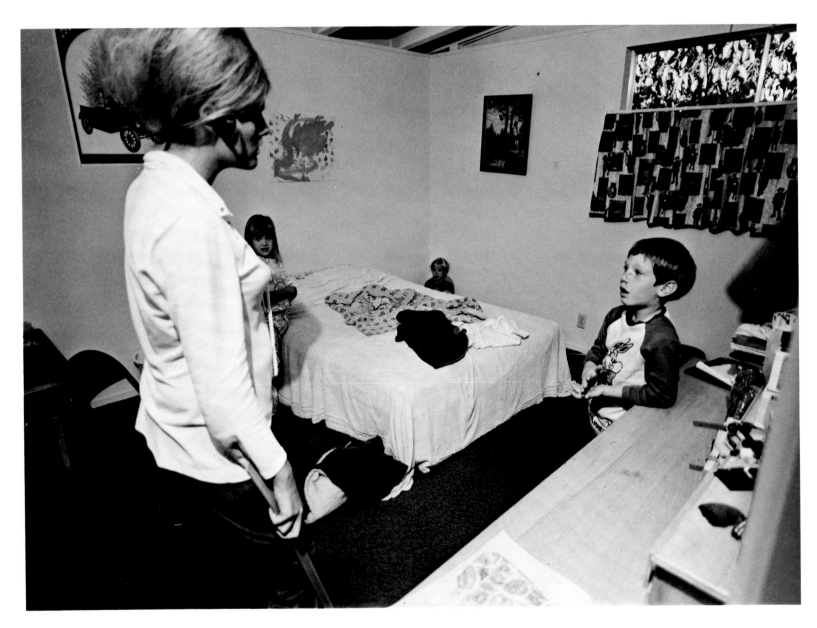

I believe in strict discipline of
my children, but they also de-
serve the right of self-explana-
tion.

Andrew doesn't like to go to
the bathroom alone.

I put it off until I can't stand it
anymore. The rottenest job in
the whole house is cleaning
the bathroom.

The best way to help your city government and have fun is to come out on a Saturday morning and pull weeds in a median strip.

It's hard to hunt because
you're always trespassing all
the housing developments
which are taking over the
open fields. Since there are
more people and more houses,
the game is moving further
out.

We're really happy. Our kids
are healthy, we eat good food
and we have a really nice
home.

I enjoy the suburbs. They provide Girl Scouts, PTA, Little League and soccer for my kids. The thing I miss most is Black cultural identity for my family. White middle-class suburbia can't supply that. Here the biggest cultural happening has been the opening of two department stores.

If Bank of America knew the truth . . .

Because we live in the sub-
burbs we don't eat too much
Chinese food. It's not avail-
able in the supermarkets so
on Saturday we eat hot dogs.

I love to cook. Meal time is the
only time the family is together. In spite of my modern
kitchen, cooking dinner for six
takes two hours. Then the kids
inhale the food in minutes.
After they are grown maybe
they will remember the meals
that their mother cooked.

This is our second annual Fourth of July block party. This year thirty-three families came for beer, barbequed chicken, corn on the cob, potato salad, green salad, macaroni salad and watermelon. After eating and drinking we staged our parade and fireworks.

My hobby is drinking. On the
weekends I enjoy getting together with my friends and
boozing.

Monday, Tuesday, Wednesday, Thursday . . . and Friday I have my hair done.

We had a cocktail party in my house for the Children's Home Society, a private adoption agency. One hundred-ninety-three people came, we charged fifty cents a drink, so we were able to make almost four hundred dollars for the Home. We believe that all children are entitled to loving parents.

We really enjoy getting together with our friends to
drink and dance. It's a wild
party and we're having a great
time.

My job as an engineer at Law-
rence Radiation Laboratory
causes a certain amount of
tension and frustration. By
running a few miles each day
I'm able to find a new sense
of being. I love running.

Fourteen years ago Dublin, California was a crossroads on U.S. 50 and Highway 21. The population was less than 1,000 (most of them cows). Today Dublin is the crossroads of Interstate Highways 580 and 680 with a population over 25,000 people. We now have fifteen gas stations, six supermarkets, two department stores and a K-Mart. And we're still growing.

I put my hair up once or twice
a week. It's the only way I can
get curls in it. When it's comb-
ed out, I'm willing to be seen
in public.

I have all the cares of home ownership and the privacy of apartment living. We have an investment in the house. So I find myself doing all the un-desirable chores to protect our investment.

Before the dissolution of our marriage my husband and I owned a bar. One day a toilet broke and we brought it home.

I bought the Doughboy pool
for David and the kids and
now no one wants to take the
responsibility for cleaning it.

My dad thinks it's a good idea to take all the leaves off the tree and rake up the yard. I think he's crazy.

We've been collecting rocks
since 1958. It's enjoyable to
get out into the open and hunt
for rocks, and it's really fun
to cut open a rock and find
a gem inside.

I don't feel that Richie playing with guns will have a negative effect on his personality. (He already wants to be a policeman). His childhood gun-playing won't make him into a cop-shooter. By playing with guns he learns to socialize with other children. I find the neighbors who are offended by Richie's gun, either the father hunts or their kids are the first to take Richie's gun and go off and play with it.

They cut down our tree forts
to put in some new houses.
We don't want houses. We
want our trees back. They
paid us five dollars to keep
people back while they cut up
the trees, but we're not going
to keep anybody out.

I believe organized sports make better citizens of children. I have four boys and they all play baseball and soccer. They learn to cooperate with others . . . and that winning isn't always the most important thing to do.

It's fun to break up the glass.
We're doing our thing for
ecology and the Boy Scouts
will give us a badge for working here.

We like to play war.

Last year I got 4 pounds of candy.

72 jelly beans
67 Candy Corns
26 Tootsie Rolls
18 Tootsie Pops
21 licorice sticks
15 jaw breakers
14 bubble gums
11 packs of gum
10 Baby Ruth bars

11 Hershey bars
4 Peter Paul Mounds bars
3 Sugar Daddies
3 pop corn balls
3 Milky Way bars
2 bags of cookies
2 salt water taffy
and a candy apple. It took me three days and I ate everything.

Washing cars is a great way
for a group of kids to make
some money.

The furniture is worn out. Don
and Tom have grown up and
soon will leave for college. Pat
will have to cook for two.

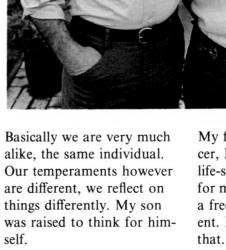

I went to Chabot Junior College and now I'm a certified chairside dental assistant. I want to work a couple of years before getting married because the number of good marriages I know I can count on two fingers.

Basically we are very much alike, the same individual. Our temperaments however are different, we reflect on things differently. My son was raised to think for himself.

My father is an ex-army officer, I'm an ex-Marine. My life-style changes were hard for my dad to understand. I'm a freer individual, not different. He doesn't understand that.

They're still going together.

Bonnie and Bob Powers

Milton and Sylvia Grissom

Jane and Norm Volponi

Aaron and Myra Latkin

Paul Dumas and Linda McPherson

Judy and Walt Hanhy

Bruce and Pat Barney

Richard and Ivy Osyerude

Ann and Mel Lemos

Janet and Lee Keene

Celia and John Baker and John Jr.

Rhonda and Joy Gilbert

Sara and Abraham Goldberg

Bill and Jeri Wilson

James and Nora Ross.

Bill and Virginia Markham

Cleo and James Pruden

Frances, John and Steve Wheelock

Joyce and Tom Abbott

Renee and Dennis Alberts

Nonie and Jerrold Schwartz

Bill and Janet Owens

Katherine and Bob Riley

We really enjoy living in a
mobile home. My hobby is
collecting coins and my wife
plays her Wurlitzer for enter-
tainment.

By having a garage sale you
can get rid of a lot of junk you
don't want. One man's junk is
another man's treasure. It's
really true.

Bill Owens' family and his in-laws.

For the last four years we
have given a caroling party.
We sing for at least forty families in our neighborhood. We
do this because we feel that
Christmas has become too
commercial.

Our house is built with the
living room in the back, so in
the evenings we sit out front
of the garage and watch the
traffic go by.

We have to move. My husband's been transferred to Southern California.

All the photographs in this book were taken with large format hand-held cameras: a Pentax 6x7, 2¼x 2¾, with three focal length lenses—55mm, 105mm and 200mm, and a Brooks Veriwide 2¼x 3¼ which was used for most of the indoor shots. It is a super wide-angle camera.

All indoor photos were taken with a fill-in flash. Sometimes I used a regular flash unit and bounced the light off the ceiling for soft-light effect. The strobe used most was a Speed Graflex bare tube. The bare tube gives a very soft, natural light effect.

The film was Tri-X, 220, rated at ASA 800. It was developed in Edwal FG-7 for around ten minutes.

All prints were made by Chong Lee of San Francisco, a very fine printer.

The book is printed in Stonetone, a two-color process by Rapaport Printing Corp., on 801b Warrens Paycote. Photoset at Rolling Stone in 11/13 pt Times Roman.